Love Letters

C B

BookLeaf Publishing
India | USA | UK

Love Letters © 2023 C B

All rights reserved.

No part of this publication may be reproduced, stored in a retrieval system, or transmitted, in any form or by any means, electronic, mechanical, photocopying, recording or otherwise, without the prior written permission of the presenters.

C B asserts the moral right to be identified as author of this work.

Presentation by *BookLeaf Publishing*

Web: www.bookleafpub.com

E-mail: info@bookleafpub.com

ISBN: 9789358734768

First edition 2023

This book is dedicated to those that will take the time to read it and absorb it. Thank you for wanting to really know me and understand me. That is the greatest gift of all - to feel seen, heard, and understood...and still loved.

ACKNOWLEDGEMENT

I want to thank every single person that has been a part of my life journey; we're all connected and we all play a role in each other's lives, even if seemingly insignificant. And I want to thank God/the universe for divinely guiding me and protecting me every step of the way.

sold "as is"

my home is for sale. it's not
perfect, but it's nice. it's
comfortable. it has natural
light radiating throughout. it has
some holes in the walls,
some stains on the floor.
some rooms are more
lively than others.
some spaces stay neglected
and even avoided.

but...if you're looking for
some sweat equity, then
this home's for you!
it needs a little TLC, but maybe
as the project-doer and
challenge-taker that you are,
this home could be a great
opportunity to build upon your
own strengths and weaknesses,
as well as, to learn about
the entire property
in the process.

strip down its walls and

uncover its old bones.
discover hidden rooms or closets,
perhaps with skeletons
lurking there, collecting dust.
a new, harmonious space will
naturally emerge by
making use of your
innate gifts to fix things.

just please don't change the
essence of the home.
please keep
the character and charm
of the home intact.
maintain its inherent value.

imagine the satisfaction
you will feel when you see
your hard work pay off,
in a house
that you can now call home.

don't miss this chance!
it won't stay on the market long!
before an investor-type buys it
and wipes out all of its
natural charm, in the
cheapest way, at the
lowest expense.

be openminded to a
project home like this one.
try to appreciate the ingenuity
in its original craft and design.
believe in its potential
and your own potential
in transforming it.
believe you can create
this dream into your reality.

being sold "as is."
located at: me, my heart, my soul [in love]

overwhelmed

stressed. drained.
the load I'm carrying is
just too heavy.
I can't think straight.
my basic needs cannot be met
by me alone.

in these heavy moments of life,
I wish I had someone to lean on.
someone that will feel me lean,
and instead of just standing strong
to support me, he will open his arms
and fully embrace me.

someone to reassure me
that it's going to be OK.
someone who understands me.
someone who truly
sees my heart,
feels my soul,
and loves me for
everything that I am,
have been,
and will be.

oh, how
I wish to be
overwhelmed in love,
than to be
overwhelmed by life.

rose-colored glasses

swooning through my
rose-colored glasses,
everything appears
the same - as love.
the world before me
glows soft and warm.

the glasses come off.
I tend to forget that
The Truth
is not the same
as how I perceive it to be
behind this
eye armor.

do I stay blinded and
pretend that I'm naive to
what these glasses are
doing to me?

love languages

sending me songs that make you think of me
feeding me the last bite of our shared dessert
making me laugh when I'm feeling grumpy
waking me up by bringing me coffee into bed
surprising me...with anything at all
opening doors for me & other acts of chivalry
cooking me dinner when I've had a long day
planning a thoughtful & special date
listening, really listening, to me
driving your vehicle around to pick me up at the entrance
bringing out my childlike innocence & wonder again
picking out special gifts for me on holidays
sensually caressing me, hugging & cuddling me
watching the stars, sunrises & sunsets together
going on adventures
exploring new places
creating special memories
having deep talks about life
calling just to say "hi" and hear my voice
leaving me a voicemail when you're tipsy
telling me how special I am to you
protecting me from danger
coddling my fragile heart when I show it to you

trusting me with your truth, too

make me the subject of your poem
write me a hand-written letter
and I'll be yours forever...

twin flame

yin and yang
black and white
sun and moon
one cannot exist without the other

the moon shines
because of the sun
reflecting off of it.
Earth - life - is
what comes between the two.

but the sun and moon exist separately,
at their own times.
never shining together,
just passing by each other
on their own paths.

we all love the radiance of the sun
and the stillness of the moon.
how could they ever shine simultaneously?

a dream job for the right guy

job title:
life partner

schedule:
full-time, forever

pay:
me.
you will have me,
forever

qualifications:
treat me as good as
I treat myself.
love me as much as
I show love to myself.
OR BETTER

training not provided for the basics of the job
(but some education can be given for certain
things)

prior experience not necessary
(DESIRE to WANT to learn is more important
than experience)

must have good references & work history
most important factor in past job history is
what you learned upon walking away from those
jobs
rather than what happened while working there...

only qualified candidates shall apply
position will remain open until the right person
is found
urgently hiring though

the "meet-cute"

I walked into the dark bar room,
full of sunken and drunken faces
numbing their pain, like
we did every weekend.

I was startled when I
heard a voice call out
from behind me.
this guy was inquisitive,
asking me my name, and
something about eighth grade.
he remembered me, and I,
him, after he spoke some more.

in that moment,
I felt truly seen.
in a room full of
random people,
my inner child was
recognized and
paid attention to.
it shook me.
I believed it to be a
divine meeting.
a real-life,

meet-cute scenario...

but I need to stop
romanticizing everything, because
while it energizes me with hopeful possibility
in the beginning, it always leaves me with
foolish despair in the end...

but...what if the
next time doesn't end in
despair, and it turns out
to be the actual meet-cute that
begins our love story?
it would be
a shame
to not begin with
hopeful possibility, then...

all aboard the chaos train

choo, choo,
the chaos train is
coming through!

more than just a train ride, it is
most likely a trainwreck,
waiting to happen.
of course,
I can't look away.
in fact, I want to step aboard
and ride it out.
but why? maybe it's the
thrill of danger, or
maybe its hoping that
I can save it from
crashing. should I risk
my own safety for the
excitement of the ride?

staying together for the kid

two separate entities,
living under one roof,
merely crossing paths.
each person independent
of the other.
no unity,
unless by force of
extended family gatherings,
which are always dreaded and
complained about.
no physical affection.
no positive interactions.
always bitter, resentful arguments
or the silent treatment
to manipulate a situation.
at war with each other.
constant tension.
is this what marriage really is?

at what point do you
choose to continue standing by your vows,
when you feel the other person is
clearly not standing by theirs?

is that what real love is?

being selfless to the point of
self-sabotage?
robbing your child of seeing
a happy marriage? or experiencing
a happy family? or seeing
her parents, happy as individuals
without having to numb
their feelings with
substances?

sometimes,
what others perceive as
the selfish thing to do, is actually
the selfless thing to do,
for the kids.

sometimes,
you break up
for the kids, too.

my family tree

drugs, booze,
cigarettes, food,
work, the news...
addictions aplenty

divorces, remarriages
abandonment, neglect

secret pregnancies, secret abortions,
struggling to get pregnant, not wanting kids

depression, anxiety,
entitlement, apathy,
self-sabotage, self-medicating,
quick temper, problems with control

multiple suicide attempts.
one suicide successful.

outsiders, loners,
people who don't belong,
martyrs of the community.
people who stand out...

a child prodigy

a nationwide hero

published authors, career musicians,
gallery-worthy artisans,
waiting-list-worthy craftsmen

teachers, veterans,
business owners, self-starters,
nurturing parents, present parents,
infectious personalities, joys to be around

greatness coexisting with chaos,
like diamonds forming under pressure.

we all choose to shine in our own way

shadows

what lurks in the shadows?
what hides in the dark?
what keeps you running
that makes you want a new start?

do not fear those mysteries
or what you do not yet know.
you must choose to know them,
and with them, you will grow.

be brave to stand up
to what the shadows hold,
for when you stand in your power,
you can turn them into gold.

see them, learn them,
and accept these parts of you.
it's for a reason that God made
the magical number two.

two animals on the ark,
yin and yang, night and day.
man and woman, hot and cold,
without the other, one cannot stay.

failure to acknowledge your shadows is neglect,
until you do, God will keep making you redirect.

celebrate them, embrace them,
even choose to show them love,
when you accept all parts of yourself,
you experience ultimate peace from above.

forever dreaming

plucking petals at pond's edge
willful wishes in the wind
skipping stones upon the sea
mystical moongazing manifesting magic
finding fairytale fantasies in everyday life
when will my Romeo reappear in reality?

love letter to my teenage self

I was just a 17-year-old kid,
asking to get a little buzzed that night.
asking to alter my mind a bit,
asking to escape my reality,
asking to have some fun with my friends,
asking to share a few laughs,
asking to listen to some music,
asking to take a few silly pictures.

I was just asking for
an ordinary night as a teenager,
living on a boring island
in the summertime.

I was just a 17-year-old kid,
I was not asking to overdose on alcohol & drugs
I was not asking to become unresponsive
I was not asking for the 25-year-old man to take advantage of me
I was not asking for the 18-year-old man to take advantage of me
I was not asking for my friends to find me incapacitated at the feet of those men
I was not asking for my friends to cover up parts of my body that were exposed

I was not asking to be life-flighted to the
hospital
I was not asking to wake up to a rape-kit being
performed on me
I was not asking to be interviewed by a detective
I was not asking to write a statement about what
I remembered

I was not asking to give away
all my clothing as "evidence,"
which included:
a pair of jeans,
a belt,
a John Deere sweatshirt,
and a Family Guy t-shirt.

I was wearing a Family Guy t-shirt.

a kid wearing a Family Guy t-shirt is not "asking
for it."

the life cycle of a wound

when you've been injured, it causes
excruciating pain sometimes.
other times, minimal pain.
if the wound is bad enough, it
may make you bleed.
sometimes severely.
other times, just a little.

when you're bleeding badly,
you must treat the wound
right away to stop the bleeding.
take necessary precautions
to heal.
you might need extra care
from doctors if the wound
is deep enough.

clean the wound.
put healing ointments on it.
protect it with a bandage.
expose it to air periodically:
let it "breathe."

taking care of the wound
will take time. and it may
hurt, sting, or ache
while it's healing.

but you must give attention to
this wound, or it will not heal properly.
you must not make the mistake of
pretending it's not there,
and that it will heal naturally on its own.
the best chance for it to heal,
and to minimize potential scarring,
is when the wound is nurtured and cared for.

over time, with proper care,
true healing occurs.
that wound turns into a scab.
then, that scab turns into a scar.

over time, you won't feel the same pain
that you felt when the injury occurred,
or during the healing process.
but the scar remains.
and with time, the scar might fade.
but you can't pretend it's not there.

the scar will always be that reminder
of the injury that happened,
the pain you felt,
the wound it gave you,
and the healing that took place,
to make that injury
forever a part of you.

the love language of the universe

open your heart to God,
and you will see, hear, and feel
all that He is trying to tell you...

He will send you wild animals on your path
He will send you repeating numbers on receipts
He will send you songs playing in the dentist's office
He will send you vanity license plates with specific messages
He will send you clouds that take meaningful shapes
He will send you overheard conversations in the grocery store
He will send you feelings in your body about certain things
He will send you angels on earth who will grace your life
He will send you coincidences...pay close attention to coincidences
He will send you nudges from the voice inside
He will send you ideas
He will send you opportunities
He will send you warning signs

He will send you messengers whom He speaks through...

He is always communicating with us.
everything has meaning.
it's up to us to stay alert and aware
to the messages He is trying to send us.
listen to Him,
follow his guidance,
and allow your life to unfold
in the best way possible,
with the universe on your side.

acceptance is key

the only way to
ultimate peace, is
through acceptance.

acceptance of
things as they are,
people as they are,
situations as they are.
allowing things to
just be.
accepting life
as it is right now,
in this present moment.

more importantly,
accepting the fact that
we have total control of
how we react to
everything in life.

we are not victims of
our circumstances forever.
we must accept that we
have the power to choose.

we must take
accountability for what
we allow to affect us.

and we must be brave enough
to choose something different if
our life circumstances
are hard to accept.

sweet girl

come here baby,
let me hold you
while you cry.

life can be unfair,
and you just don't
understand why.

you want someone to listen
and really be there for you,
not just when you do something good,
but unconditionally, all the time,
no matter what you do.

you deserve that attention,
sweet girl.
your heart is so giving.
you're full of so much love,
it's what makes your life worth living.

never settle for anything less,
than the love you have inside of you.
for you are worthy of that kind of love,
and it's that love that will get you through.

surrender (a song)

how much can a person take?
please God get me out of this place.
pure disrespect to my face
at every turn, from every person,
that comes my way.

the tale they tell is not my truth.
I will never believe their lies, I refuse.
I've been through hell, I've paid my dues.
but I'm not perfect and I have no excuse.

so I surrender
to my karma and my journey
it's not always pleasant,
but I am always learning.
for a happy ending,
I will always be yearning.
I just want to be loved,
but I only end up hurting.

misunderstood should be my middle name.
we are not the same kids
as we were in tenth grade.
I've grown and I've changed,
I don't want this small town fame.

any more and I will surely go insane.

how much longer can I just keep existing?
how much longer can I just keep resisting?
the urge inside to see more and explore
get out of dodge and learn what I'm here for...

so I surrender
to the karma and my journey.
it might not always be pleasant,
but I will always keep learning.
for a happy ending, I will
still always be yearning.
I will find true love and
I won't end up hurting.

alone but not lonely

I can pick my own flowers.
I can buy my own gifts.
I can take myself on dates.
I can enjoy those things alone.
and sometimes, I prefer it.

but I don't want to
do it alone all the time...

do I really enjoy it,
or is it just
what I've always
been used to?

ready to jump

teetering on the edge.
looking over at what lies below.
I'm terrified
but at the same time,
thrilled.

I've been standing here
far too long,
overthinking everything
that can go wrong.
second-guessing myself,
wondering if I should back away
from the edge instead.

what I've learned
while I've been here
standing tall, is that
when it feels scary to jump...
that's exactly when you do.
embrace the fear,
jump with all your might,
and cannonball
into the next phase
of your life!

thirty-one

year of fun
year of sun
year of life has just begun

year of done
year of won
year of settling for none,
hun

Printed in the USA
CPSIA information can be obtained
at www.ICGtesting.com
LVHW011500120624
782915LV00015B/752

9 789358 734768